Living and Non-living in the Desert

Rebecca Rissman

Raintree is an imprint of Capstone Global Library Limited, a company incorporated in England and Wales having its registered office at 7 Pilgrim Street, London, EC4V 6LB – Registered company number: 6695582

www.raintreepublishers.co.uk
myorders@raintreepublishers.co.uk

Text © Capstone Global Library Limited 2014
First published in hardback in 2014
Paperback edition first published in 2015
The moral rights of the proprietor have been asserted.

Edited by Daniel Nunn, Rebecca Rissman, and Catherine Veitch
Designed by Cynthia Della-Rovere
Picture research by Tracy Cummins
Production by Sophia Argyris
Originated by Capstone Global Library Ltd
Printed and bound in China by Leo Paper Products Ltd

ISBN 978 1 406 26588 0 (hardback)
17 16 15 14 13
10 9 8 7 6 5 4 3 2 1

ISBN 978 1 406 26595 8 (paperback)
18 17 16 15 14
10 9 8 7 6 5 4 3 2 1

British Library Cataloguing in Publication Data
A full catalogue record for this book is available from the British Library.

Acknowledgements
We would like to thank the following for permission to reproduce photographs: Alamy p. 12 (© Bill Gozansky); istockphoto pp. 1 (© Erik Bettini), 21 (© Paul Erickson); Shutterstock pp. 4, 23a (© Junker), 5 (© SNEHIT), 6, 23b (© hagit berkovich), 7 (© EcoPrint), 8 (© Jan Kratochvila), 9 (© Igor Janicek), 10, 23c (© orxy), 11 © Worachat Sodsri), 13 (© urosr), 14, 23d (© Galyna Andrushko), 15 (© LouLouPhotos), 16 (© Vladimir Wrangel), 17 (© taelove7), 18 (© Patrick Poendl), 19 (© Fatseyeva), 22 (© Anton Prado PHOTO); Superstock p. 20 (© Minden Pictures).

Front cover photograph of a thorny devil, crossing cracked mud in Australia reproduced with permission of Getty Images (© Minden Pictures).

We would like to thank Michael Bright and Diana Bentley for their invaluable help in the preparation of this book.

Every effort has been made to contact copyright holders of material reproduced in this book. Any omissions will be rectified in subsequent printings if notice is given to the publisher.

All the Internet addresses (URLs) given in this book were valid at the time of going to press. However, due to the dynamic nature of the Internet, some addresses may have changed, or sites may have changed or ceased to exist since publication. While the author and publisher regret any inconvenience this may cause readers, no responsibility for any such changes can be accepted by either the author or the publisher.

Some words are in bold, **like this**.
You can find them in the glossary on page 23.

Contents

What is a desert?

A desert is a dry **habitat**.

Many deserts are very hot during the day and cold at night.

Different types of plants and animals live in the desert.

There are **non-living** things in the desert, too.

What are living things?

Living things are alive. Living things need air and **sunlight**. Living things need food and water.

Living things grow and change.

Living things move on their own.

What are non-living things?

Non-living things are not alive. Non-living things do not need air and **sunlight**.

Non-living things do not need food or water.

Non-living things do not grow and change on their own.

Non-living things do not move on their own.

Is a rock living or non-living?

A rock does not need food or water.

A rock does not need air and **sunlight**.

A rock does not move on its own.

A rock does not grow or change on its own.

A rock is **non-living**.

Is a lizard living or non-living?

A lizard needs food and water.

A lizard moves on its own.

A lizard grows and changes.

A lizard needs air and **sunlight**.

A lizard is **living**.

Is a cactus living or non-living?

A cactus grows and changes.

A cactus moves on its own towards the sun.

A cactus needs water.

A cactus needs air and **sunlight**.

A cactus is **living**.

Is sand living or non-living?

Sand does not move on its own.

Sand does not grow and change on its own.

Sand does not need food or water.

Sand does not need air and **sunlight**.

Sand is **non-living**.

Is a camel living or non-living?

A camel grows and changes.

A camel moves on its own.

A camel needs food and water.

A camel needs air and **sunlight**.

A camel is **living**.

Is a spider living or non-living?

A spider moves on its own.

A spider needs food and water.

A spider grows and changes.

A spider needs air and **sunlight**.

A spider is **living**.

What do you think?

Is this soil **living** or **non-living**?

Glossary

 **habitat** place where plants and animals live

 **living** alive. Living things need food and water. They breathe and move on their own. They grow and change.

 **non-living** not alive. Non-living things do not need food or water. They do not move on their own. They do not grow and change on their own.

 **sunlight** light from the sun

Find out more

Websites

Click through these images of living and non-living things, then take a quiz!
www.bbc.co.uk/schools/scienceclips/ages/5_6/ourselves.shtml

Look for eight living things in this pond scene!
www.bbc.co.uk/schools/scienceclips/ages/8_9/habitats.shtml

Check out this site to learn more about what living things need.
www.kidsbiology.com/biology_basics/needs_living_things/living_things_have_needs1.php

Books

A Desert Habitat (Introducing Habitats), Kelley MacAulay and Bobbie Kalman (Crabtree, 2006)

Desert Animals (American Habitats), Connor Dayton (Powerkids Press, 2009)

Living and Nonliving, Carol K. Lindeen (Capstone Press, 2008)

Index